I'm Going To **READ!**™

These levels are meant only as guides;
you and your child can best choose a book that's right.

Level 1: Kindergarten–Grade 1 . . . Ages 4–6

- word bank to highlight new words
- consistent placement of text to promote readability
- easy words and phrases
- simple sentences build to make simple stories
- art and design help new readers decode text

Level 2: Grade 1 . . . Ages 6–7

- word bank to highlight new words
- rhyming texts introduced
- more difficult words, but vocabulary is still limited
- longer sentences and longer stories
- designed for easy readability

Level 3: Grade 2 . . . Ages 7–8

- richer vocabulary of up to 200 different words
- varied sentence structure
- high-interest stories with longer plots
- designed to promote independent reading

Level 4: Grades 3 and up . . . Ages 8 and up

- richer vocabulary of more than 300 different words
- short chapters, multiple stories, or poems
- more complex plots for the newly independent reader
- emphasis on reading for meaning

LEVEL 3

Library of Congress Cataloging-in-Publication Data Available

6 8 10 9 7

Published by Sterling Publishing Co., Inc.
387 Park Avenue South, New York, NY 10016
Text copyright © 2005 by Harriet Ziefert Inc.
Illustrations copyright © 2005 by Lionel Kalish
Distributed in Canada by Sterling Publishing
c/o Canadian Manda Group, 165 Dufferin Street
Toronto, Ontario, Canada M6K 3H6
Distributed in Great Britain and Europe by Chris Lloyd at Orca Book
Services, Stanley House, Fleets Lane, Poole BH15 3AJ, England
Distributed in Australia by Capricorn Link (Australia) Pty. Ltd.
P.O. Box 704, Windsor, NSW 2756, Australia

I'm Going To Read is a trademark of Sterling Publishing Co., Inc.

Sterling ISBN-13: 978-1-4027-2105-2

For information about custom editions, special sales, premium and
corporate purchases, please contact Sterling Special Sales
Department at 800-805-5489 or specialsales@sterlingpub.com.

I'm Going To
READ!™

When Daddy Had the Chicken Pox

Pictures by Lionel Kalish

STERLING

New York / London
www.sterlingpublishing.com/kids

I
had the
chicken pox.

My sister
had the
chicken pox.

My brother
had the
chicken pox.

Then Daddy got the chicken pox.

Daddy had fever.
Daddy had a headache.
Daddy had a rash.

Daddy felt sick.
Very sick.

Daddy was too sick
to watch TV.
Or read the newspaper.

When Mommy brought him lunch,
he didn't want it.
But she said he had to drink.

Daddy couldn't come
to my ballet recital.
Mommy came by herself.

I missed Daddy.
I was sad.
I didn't smile.

"When will Daddy get better?"
I asked.

"When he stops getting new pox,"
Mommy said.
"That's when he'll feel better."

We all wanted to see
Daddy's pox.

Daddy looked terrible—
all covered with pox.
"Yikes!"

Daddy scratched.
"I'm itchy!"

I said, "Don't scratch.
Or you'll get scars."

Paul said, "Maybe a bath
will help Daddy."

Mommy called the doctor.
The doctor said, "Have
him take an oatmeal bath."

Daddy soaked in the tub—
just like the doctor said.

I wanted to help.
But Mommy said no.
So I went to my room.

Daddy was sick for four days.
I was scared—
scared Daddy might have
to go to the hospital.

Every night
before I went to sleep
I begged for Daddy
to get better.

One morning
Daddy started
giving orders.

"Where is everyone?"

"Bring me the newspaper!"

"Bring me the
remote control!"

Bring my briefcase!"

"Bring a cheese
sandwich!"

Daddy was getting better!

Daddy could build with me.
We made a hospital
on top of his briefcase.

The next morning Daddy
ate breakfast with us.
"Sit up straight,"
he said to me.

"And after breakfast
let's have a ballet recital
in the living room."

Mommy and Daddy sat
on the sofa.

And I danced.

Everything was good again!